I0450087

A SAGA OF POEMS

Youthful Heart of Poetry

MICHAEL R. GREGO
EDITED BY MARY C. CANTWELL

authorHOUSE®

AuthorHouse™
1663 Liberty Drive, Suite 200
Bloomington, IN 47403
www.authorhouse.com
Phone: 1-800-839-8640

© 2007 Michael R. Grego Edited by Mary C. Cantwell. All rights reserved.

No part of this book may be reproduced, stored in a retrieval system, or
transmitted by any means without the written permission of the author.

First published by AuthorHouse   8/3/2007

ISBN: 978-1-4343-0663-0 (sc)

Printed in the United States of America
Bloomington, Indiana

This book is printed on acid-free paper.

*This book is dedicated
to my Heavenly Father
without His Grace I would not be here.*

Table of Contents

A saga of poems by Michael Grego, written before 2003.
Edited by Mary C. Cantwell

Poems by Michael Grego and Mary C. Cantwell, written after June 2003.

A Black Slip of Rejection

I need to get you off of my mind.
The length of time allotted
for thinking about you
has long since expired.
You are not as easy to get over
as you may believe.
Anyone that has had you,
and lost you,
would surely know.

I still insisted on interface
and conversation from a relationship
that, I knew, just couldn't be.

I have tried to speak with you
in a way that you could hear and comprehend.
Yet you still pay no mind to my cry.
I reached out for your hand in friendship.
You gave me a sword;
a cursed, black slip of rejection.

A Lover's Dream

Lust, not love, is most lovers' overture.
Lust is a fantasy;
as a lover cannot find love in lust.
Lust is to love
as a fairy tale is to a non-fiction.
Therefore lust is a fable where love is truth.

Lust is a love's introduction to dreams.
A lover is a dreamer.
A dreamer's reverie ought not be composed
of lust, it should be composed of love.

A lover's lust encourages
the desire of being loved.
It's the harmonious background
with the desire of being loved.

Thus a lover's lust is the desperate
background melody searching for love.
A lover's lust will fade as love flourishes.
Therefore a lover's lust is
a lover's fateful finale.

Arm in Arm

The moment has arrived.
This image, it seems, has forever been
in my mind.
The night is here. I'm waiting for her arrival.
I see her.
The sight of her is almost more than I can bear.
My eyes are blinded by her beauty.
Never have I seen anything so beautiful.
I am joyous. I shall dance.

I shall dance with ecstasy, as well as
Contentment, for she is in my arms,
and I'll always be in hers.
I wish this moment would never end.
I shall not allow it's ending in my mind.
It shall stay with me for all eternity.

The night is almost over,
though we wish it wasn't.
The night glimmers with stars;
the moon, brightly shining.
The closing song has begun.
Neither of us want this moment to end.

It 's almost like a dream.
I expect to wake up,
and find out that it was only my imagination.
The night is over,
but the feelings shall forever
remain in my heart.

I'm in her arms.
Wishes are spoken
that each other may stay,
but it's not to be.
The night is over
and parting is certain.
Separate ways we go
with the hope
that we may meet again.

Sleepless Nights

Night after night
I find myself awake in my bed,
all the lights turned out
and the ceiling looming overhead.

Darkness surrounds me.
I often find myself
pacing the floor
in a deep terrible cold sweat.
Looking all around, I realize
you are nowhere near.
In my despair
I hold my face in my hands.
I can feel the tears
building behind my closed eyes.

Before allowing myself to brake out in tears,
I try to slumber once again.
Not near asleep,
Staring at the ceiling
I remember how much I miss
the time we've spent together;
how much I miss you.

Night after night it happens,
again and again.
My mind's confused.
I can't help but think about you.

You're always on my mind.

You are on my mind
and that won't change.

That will not change for all eternity.

Miss You

I don't get to see you
as often as I wish.
You should know that
you are someone whom I miss very much.
I don't need the assurance
of seeing you every day.
I just need the promise
of being able to talk to you
and share everything with you.
Your voice is so soft;
smooth, soothing, comforting
and so unforgettable.

We understand each other
well enough that no matter how long
we're apart, we can pick up
exactly where we left off.

It's true that I don't get to see you
as often as I'd like.
I hope that the time we've spent together
was as good for you as it was for me.

A Phone Call

When the news was broken to me
a stream of tears flowed
as water along a river's bank
and now is furiously tumbling
from my heart.

Why does it have to be this way?

A phone call - the dreaded phone call;
One that has truly changed my life
forever.
If the call had not been made,
My beloved would still be in my life.
A phone call - the dreaded phone call;
I will regret it ever happening.
I shall miss my beloved,
and hope that I'll be missed by her.

I guess it was just too good to be true.
I'll not mourn the time that was
spent with her.
My tears will dry
as the riverbed in summer.
I will sit here, now, and ponder
in my sorrow and my endless misery.
Farewell, my love.

The Choice Has Been Made

She's beautiful;
too beautiful for the likes of me.
The day will come when she realizes
that she's too good for someone like me.
I sit and wait for that time to come.

That time will be the dreaded of all times, and
when it comes I know not what I will do.
I know that the time is drawing closer.
Little did I know; that time is NOW.

I have waited for it for quite a while,
Yet, still, when it came, it was unexpected.
I have been replaced by another man
who caught her eye just as she caught his.

I know now that I'll only be second best.
The choice has been made.
I can't lay blame on anyone.
For the choice was only hers to make.
She will love and be loved by another.
I shall miss my love, forever.
Farewell my love;
I guess it just wasn't meant to be.

I'm Sorry

My dear beloved, I have lost you.
I know not your thoughts,
nor your feelings.
But the way you looked at me
told me that we were truly
just not meant to be together.

I may have been ignorant
about your thoughts, and your feelings.
I may have been incompetent
about pleasing you.
I might have overlooked or missed
clues, hints, or nudges.

Maybe my ignorance was an excuse
for not wanting to accept the obvious.
I am sorry if my incompetence
has made this difficult on you as well.
My failure to notice your feelings has
made accepting the reality
problematic for the both of us.

I see now, that I allowed myself
to get too attached to you.
I still don't know the meaning
of your departure.
Will I ever know?
What's for the best remains unknown.

If There's A Positive

Maybe there are some positives
that came out of this relationship.
I don't know.

> *I don't know about her,*
> *but I'll never love someone,*
> *as I loved her,*
> *I'll not let myself get*
> *that involved again.*

Again, I'm glad that she ended it sooner,
rather then later.
The ending might have been more dramatic
if it had been later.

> *Later I was glad the choice was made*
> *before I fell head over heels in love.*

In love, had we been more attached,
it would have been more complicated.
I didn't end the relationship and I see
she had no other choice.

> *No other choice would make it any worse.*
> *I don't think it could have been.*
> *Nothing she can say will hurt me anymore.*

Anymore, we both know what we want
In our future relationships.

> *In future relationships, maybe I will open up*
> *and love again.*
> *I am devastated this had to happen to me.*

Although there may be something positive
> *that came out of this relationship,*
> > *it will always be outweighed*
> > > *by the negative of her departure.*

Heaven On Earth

To me, being with you is
like being in heaven.
You are the most beautiful woman
that I have ever seen.
You caught my eye
just as your presence turns heads
when you walk down the street.
The sky is at its brightest blue, and
the lake water shines crystal clear
when I am in your presence.

When you walk down the street,
the trees seem fuller
and when you are sad
the earth seems to follow.
With your sadness
the planet seems to stop rotating.
The world is featureless
when you don't smile.
So my wish for you is happiness.

Without you, my life would be worth nothing.
Everything is brighter when you are around.
When you are leaning up against me
I never want to move.
When your arms are around me
I never want to let go.
The joy of you being with me in that sense
is like heaven on earth.

Only A Dream

A dream is just a dream
and surely can't be a reality.
For as you know my dream is of her.
Night after night,
the same dream
again and again.
All dreams have a beginning
and an ending.

I sit under a tree
in what seems endless misery,
as a shadow emerges in front of me.
I lift my head off my knees
to catch a short glimpse of who it is.
The shadow is only visible,
for the sun is behind her.
It is a woman, but who could she be?
As I sit there in the shadow
I think of the possibilities.
My eyes are blinded by the sunlight
and in that short time,
the shadowed figure is directly over me.

Now I can make out her face.
It's my beloved,
whom I have missed so very much.
"Has my dream come true?"
is what is running through my head,
as she sits down next to me.
She whispers to me
with her soft smooth voice,
"I am sorry. Forgive me."
I don't know what to expect.
For in a dream, what is the reality?

All dreams have an ending
and this one was ideal.
A dream is a dream
and truth is truth
and dreams sometimes do come true.

Through Her Eyes

I put myself in her shoes because
I didn't understand her thoughts.
And now that I have looked through her eyes
I am sorry.
Now I know the reasons for her departure.

I teased her and taunted her.
I don't know how or why
she put up with me.
And I don't want to know,
for it would more than likely
drive me to tears.

I acted as if obsessed with her
and I frightened her.
I am truly sorry.
I have done things deliberately
that she specifically told me not to do,
and I am remorseful.
I made her cry.
And for that, I am especially ashamed.

I know I can't say "sorry" enough
but I hope she can at least
acknowledge my apology.
If she feels she can never to talk to me again,
I will truly understand.
Now I realize
what she's dealt with, all this time.

Like a Rose

A red rose is so beautiful
in its natural state
as she is naturally beautiful.
She is like a red rose so full and rich.
Her beauty is unique and rare.
There are no souls alive
that truly appreciate her beauty.
The beauty on the outside
is just as important
as the beauty on the inside.
With that said,
I must tell you she has both.
Her ideas are so colorful
and so full of life.
Her personality cannot be matched.
Her face and her soul must be treasured.
Both her inner beauty
and her outer beauty
shall be cherished forever.
But unlike a rose
whose beauty is short lived,
her beauty shall never die.

A Gift

It is a gift that you receive,
the gift of my caring for you.
This gift is worth a great deal to me.
It is something we all need.

I am not one to take things back,
and I know that you are aware of this.

I will say you have a choice:
you may deny your feelings
and throw this gift away.
But I think you perceive my notions
that you are worth it.
Yes, you are worth it.

Now, it's your turn to share the gift.

As Snow Falls

Flake by flake
snow falls from the heavens.
Its texture smooth and soft-looking.
Each flake is unique,
similar to life's distinctive qualities.
Each flake is so precious
and yet so fragile.
A snowflake birthed white and pure
dropping from the sky,
just like a child's mind and soul are pure
when birthed from it's mother's womb.

And now the flakes fall
as night approaches.
When they reach the farthest depths,
and the deepest darkness,
they suddenly come upon their fate:
the flakes are no more.
They have melted.

Is life unlike the snowfall?
Doesn't life plummet us about,
up and down,
as if we were riding on the wind?
And we find that time is of the essence?

Just as the snow is whirled about
and melts rapidly,
life is similarly measured.
Some may see the snow fall, but
for me, the snow is melting.

Just Forget

I know why you cry.
I know it was me.
I am sorry for what I did.
I hope you will be able to just forget.
I'll never make that mistake again.

But think, perhaps there is a reason
for the mistake being made.
Maybe I have worn out my welcome
and I am sorry.
I'll always miss you being part of my life.

So please waste no tears on me.
I have been distraught ever since that day.
For me, when tears start to fall
they'll not stop 'til the cause is resolved.
That said, I feel I'll forever be in tears.
A life with you would be
too good to be true.

For a second chance
is not what I am going to receive.
The second chance is only in my dreams,
and dreams rarely come true.
Again, it would be better for you
to forget about us,
and what we ever were.

As your life moves on so shall mine.

Confused

I am confused.
Making choices has not been my strong suit.
I wish I were not feeling this way.

I had to let her know the break might be coming,
Our situation has been complicated
by many things.

My mind has been filled with several thoughts and many feelings:
        Do we stay friends?   Continue to date?
                Is marriage in our future?
            Is this really love?
                    Does she feel the same way I do?

I don't know what is next.
There is so much yet to be figured out,
let alone resolved.
I don't know my next action.
Time alone is what I need.

                            I have been doing some serious thinking
                                    for quite some time now,
                                and still, I can't say its over.
                        Situations such as these are not easy.
                            Although I am still confused,
                            I am left at a loss for words.
                            A commitment such as this
                            is not one to be taken lightly.

A Walk Through The Seasons

As we walk through winter
we leave imprints on the snow.
As we walk through summer
we leave tracks in the sand.
As we walk through the fall
we leave a trace of our path in the leaves.
As we walk through the spring
we leave our shadow behind in the sun.

Each season allows us to leave
a physical imprint on the world.
Just as when we walk through life
we leave impressions in people's minds.
Life is all about good first impressions.
The legacy you leave is created by
the impact you make on others.

Leave a good legacy,
make a good first impression
as you walk through the seasons of life.

A Sudden Change
in Temperature

I am so relaxed when I am around you.
It is like being in a steamy shower.
The water is heated
gradually to perfection.
The water is warm and soothing.
I am in a deep daze.

Then, suddenly, someone opens the door
and all the steam escapes the room.
The hot water turns to ice water
and I am shivering.
I am almost frozen,
fingers, turning blue.
I am shocked into a return to reality.

All I can think about
is how much I miss you
and how I can't stand being away from you.
I am devastated without you.

tragedy

you may even find yourself
thinking of utter tragedy.
    after all,
    tragedy is only a mere formality
    of how your mind deals
    with problems and hard decisions.
        quickly
        I grab the covers
        and throw them
        over my trembling body.

my mind is telling me
that life for me is full of darkness.
    the fear of being unprepared
    for an unexpected tragedy.

An Unexpected Tragedy

A sharp ice cold chill down my spine
    Trembling
        Freezing
            Tingling
Staring into the bottomless dark.
Amazing what you see when it is pitch black.
    Skin crawling
        Love
            Hate
The hair on my arms stands up.
    Jet black room
        Frightened
            Shivering
                Unprepared
                    Depressing
                        Alone
                Scared
            Abandoned
        Cramped
      Demonstrative
  Out of control
My mind, a pit of darkness
    Tragedy
        Confined.

    It's amazing
    what you can see in complete darkness.
        It's amazing
        what you can hear in utter silence.
    It's amazing
    what you think of when you can't see or hear.

Alone In Life

I turn out the lights and shut the door
as I am about to hit the floor.
I stumble as I head toward my bed.
I throw my tense, apprehensive body and soul
on top of my covers.
I relax and sink into the cushions.

Sudden sharp ice cold chills
course down my spine.
My muscles tense up
and my body thrusts forward in a tight cringe.
The hairs on my arm stand up
and quiver as the cold seems to stream
through my veins.
I am trembling.
My body instantly curls into a ball.
My body temperature continues to fall.

I find myself seeing unusual things.
I am amazed
at what I can see in complete darkness,
Staring into the abyss
dots and waves of different sizes
flowing together before my eyes.
All are represented with their own brilliance
and distinguishing colors.
The astonishing figures
suddenly seem to flow together
like euphoric music.

I'm amazed at what I can hear
in complete silence.
A loud arousing ringing of a melody
through my head.

Suddenly the harmonic melody
and brilliant colors that are being displayed
across my mind are turning weary and tedious.
I am realizing the severity of my current situation.
My skin is starting to crawl
as I think of being confined.
Fear races though my mind.
The panic of being abandoned by life.
The horror of hatred toward life
more specifically toward my own life.
The feeling of being trapped
within my own mind.
I am falling fast
down into the deep endless pit of my own insanity.
I am devastated
at what I think of when I am all alone.
I find myself thinking of utter catastrophe.
After all,
tragedy is only
a mere formality of how my mind
deals with certain situations.
My mind isn't ready.
The time has come and
I'm not ready.

Calm Ocean Waters
for Laura

Lying under the glimmering stars
and the glamorous moon,
rocking back and forth; up and down,
waves strike quietly against the hull.
The moon reflects the ocean's crystal clear waters.
The sea is a deep dark blue.
The breeze is calm,
but comfortable and smooth.
There is the faint smell of salt in the air,
not unpleasant.
It is so quiet and peaceful.

This moment is so perfect and so exhilarating.
You are wishing as you look up at the stars
for someone with whom to share this sublime moment.
As you look around you see no one.
There is not another soul for thousands of miles.
It is so disturbing and so eerie.

It doesn't matter where you are on earth
if you have no one with you
to experience and share the moment
it becomes pointless and wasted.

Don't go through life without someone by your side,
someone with whom to share life's possibilities.
It makes the journey easier and more enjoyable.
The right person will come.
You have to be ready.

I wish you a good life.
I wish you success in all of your endeavors.
Take life one step at a time
and you will get through it just fine.
Fare thee well.

Biggest Regret

Everyday I will regret
giving up so easily on you.

The world seemed so right
when you were around.
Everything was brighter
when you were near.

I will miss your full and beautiful smile
And your deep, lovely blue eyes.

I'll long for your voice,
so silky, smooth and soothing.
I'll miss your soft, relaxing touch.
Your face, so innocent and pure,
was just a joy to touch.

When your arms were around me
I never wanted to move.
Your beauty and your personality would grow
more and more brilliant.

You have been my greatest desire.
Maybe I should confront you about it?
NO!!!
I am never speaking up again.
It only hurt me.
I'd rather it be a mystery
than your deserting me.
I am never speaking up again,
Starting now!
I will always regret giving up on you.

October

Tastes:

Halloween candy
Pumpkin pie
Home cooked meals

Smells:

Turkey roasting, corn boiling, squash baking
Leaves soaked in mildew on the ground
Slightly smoky from the wood in the fire

Sounds:

The wood crackling in the stove
Leaves rustling on the ground
The wind as it blows your jacket around you
Kids laughing and playing in the leaves
Doorbell ringing every two or three minutes

Sights:

Friends, ringing the bell, visiting
Children playing in the yard
Leaves dropping from the tallest trees
Cooler nights, sunny days
Shades of leaves

Recovery
By Mary Cantwell for Michael Grego

*HE SITS IN A CHAIR... **TRAPPED!***
HIS WORDS
     FALL
        FROM
           HIS
              FINGERS...
***EXPLODING** ON THE SCREEN!*
HIS SMILE IS INFECTIOUS.
IT BRIGHTENS MY DAY.
HIS LIFE'S BEEN CHANGED
     FROM WHAT HE ONCE KNEW.
YET HE GOES ON...
HE STRUGGLES...
     WITH MEMORY,
        WITH STANDING,
           WITH BREATHING...
HE SHINES...
     WITH JOY,
        WITH LOVE,
           WITH HOPE...

     HE LEARNS ONCE AGAIN.

A Valentine's Day
Poem for Mom

Yearly we celebrate Valentines' Day;
A day to remember; a caring day.
A day to give your husband or wife
A lot of love reflecting your life.
A day to give your mom or dad
A poem about the life you've had.

Valentines' Day is for young and old,
For lovers, friends, the shy and the bold.
We give cards and gifts, candy and flowers.
All to demonstrate warm feelings of ours!

So on this Valentines' Day, Mom, I wanted to say:
I'm thankful for you each and every day.
I love you more than words can say.
And I tell you now on this special day!

MY ENEMY

ANGER BOILS INSIDE OF ME.
THE CHAIR IS MY ENEMY.
PAIN FROM SHARPNESS BURNS INSIDE OF
ME.
WHERE IS THE END
OF THIS AGONY?

HEAR ME

PEOPLE THINK THAT THEY HEAR ME.
WORDS COME
THROUGH MY FINGERS.
PAIN AND CONFUSION…
WHERE DID THE OLD LIFE GO?
LISTEN TO ME.
LISTEN TO MY WORDS.
HEAR ME.
HEAR ME.

THE MAN IN THE CHAIR

THE MAN SITS IN THE CHAIR.
DO I KNOW HIM?
THE LOVE IS PALPABLE
COMING FROM HIS HEART.
CAN YOU HEAR HIS LOVE?
I HEAR IT IN HIS VOICE,
IN HIS BREATHING,
IN HIS SLEEP…
LOVE IS LIKE THAT.
IT PERMEATES THE AIR I BREATHE.
THE MAN IS THE REAL DAD
WHO LOVES ME.

Senses of Spring

A time of change;
Warm days, longer days
introducing cooler nights;
Sleeping with the windows open;
A sudden storm crops up;
Hearing the rain patter on the roof;
Breezes flowing through the treetops;
Bringing the senses to abrupt attention.

Senses reeling
with sounds, sights, and scents of Spring.
I hear the rumble of far off thunder
telling me that the rain is not far away.
Nightsounds creep in the open windows:
Bugs droning, voices murmuring,
Leaves rustling in the breeze,
The hum of distant traffic as it moves
along the freeway,
The screech of an owl
as it stalks it scurrying prey.

Visions of spring assault the senses:
The bright green of newly blossoming trees
Flowers in bloom, colors of spring,
Lilac, pink, white, golden, colors that splatter
across my eyes.

The fluttering of colorful butterflies
as they quiver above the flowers;
Watching white billowing clouds
drift across the bluest of skies;
The rebirth of wildlife
as the new youngsters scamper
across the lawn;
Watching the farmers
planting their crops for another season.

Scents redolent of spring:
The earth as it is turned for the plow;
The smell of rain in the air
promising an evening shower;
And bringing the odor of worms
climbing out of the earth
to catch the rain drops;
A trace of the bouquet of lilacs
drifts across the yard.

Springtime,
a comfortable time for me;
A time for rebirth and renewal;
A time for bright colors
and clean fresh scents;
A time to find a new beginning.
Do you feel the same?

Loving Scents

NURTURING SMELLS
COMING FROM THE KITCHEN.
LAUGHTER AND COOKIES;
DINNER ON THE TABLE.
MOMS SHARE THEIR HEARTS
WHEN THEY SHARE THEIR TABLE WITH US.
LOVE IN THE SHAPE OF
A CHOCOLATE CHIP COOKIE!

ANGER

White hot heat burns into my soul.
Feelings so searing I believe I may ignite.
Do I act out my fury?
Do I keep it a prisoner inside of me?
Where does the anger come from?
Who will help me in my time of need?
Who will help me douse these flames?
Or must I suffer this heat alone?

MY STRENGTH

SHE CARRIES THE WEIGHT OF MY BODY,
THE WEIGHT OF MY SOUL.

MY PAIN IS HER PAIN.
MY JOY IS HER JOY.
SHE IS THE EVER-PRESENT PRESENCE
IN MY RECOVERY.

SHE IS STRENGTH.
SHE IS LOVE.
SHE IS MY MOTHER.

SANITY

LAUGHTER KEEPS ME SANE.
A TEASING GESTURE…
A GIGGLE…   A GUFFAW…
THE MAN IN THE CHAIR
*   LAUGHS WITH ME.*
HE OFFERS HUMOR
*   WHEN THERE IS DESPAIR.*
IT'S LAUGHTER THAT KEEPS ME SANE.
MY DAD IS THE ONE
*   WHO MAKES ME LAUGH.*

Friendship
Dedicated to my friend, Tiffany Johnson

Needed by all…
Not too hard to find…
A special person in your life…
You're comfortable around her.
She's someone to help you through the hard times.
You share almost everything with her.
Someone to party with…
Someone to support you…
Someone to get advice from…
She would never put you down in any way.

You may meet this special someone
          in some of the oddest or ordinary places:
Like at school, at work or
          you may run into her in a public place.
Once you make a friend
          you need to work on keeping that friendship.
Be kind to each other…
Be there for them…
Support them through the hard times
Enjoy the good times, together.

And when apart
You will feel the sadness, and discomfort…
          But you'll know that a true friend
                              isn't ever far away.

Comfortable

His name is Sirus, "my cat",
    the biggest cat I've ever known.
Comfortable...watching him lie
    on the kitchen chair,
    his bobbed tail folded within.
He fills the ample seat
    curled into a huge furry ring of contentment.
He sleeps through the day.
Comfortable…as I lean over to pat
    his generous coat.
Relaxing, he moves his body
    to where he wants me to pet him
    secure in the knowledge that I'll be gentle
    and give him what he wants.
Comfortable…when he jumps onto my lap,
    cozy in his manner,
    curling to a ball of fur so I can pet him.
Comfort…he brings to me
    allowing me the intimacy of friendship
    even though he's as independent
    as his bob cat ancestors.
Calm… he brings to me
    as I pat his softness and feel his warmth
    listening to his slow breathing
    leaving me aware that he is always there for me.
Comfortable…as I stroke his fur,
    his tongue slides out of his mouth,
    a silly sign of his own contentment.
Comfortable…we both are,
    happy to share our lives
    Sirus, my cat.

Dating

You've known each other for a while.
You've finally reached a comfort level
to ask her out on a date.
Now that you feel close enough to her,
you push your relationship up a notch.
Being close to someone you respect
and showing that you care about her
is a very affirming thing.

Now the question is
finding the right place to take her.
The decision depends on
how much you like her.

If you very much like her
then you should bring her some pretty flowers
and take her somewhere fancy
like the Eagle's Nest.
If you like her a little less
then you might want to go
to a casual restaurant
such as Steak'n Shake.

After dinner you may be thinking
about another place to go.
You may be flooded with choices
such as going to a romantic movie;
or going to a ballroom to dance the night away;
or go to a sporting event or the symphony.
You may take her to a national park
to run in the crunchy, colorful leaves
that cascade from the trees,

or sledding when the weather's
crisp and cold.
Pack a tasty picnic lunch
and take her to a lake or a swimming pool
for a quick dip on a hot summer's day.
Or on a windy spring day,
find a kite and watch it take flight.

After your day or evening
invite her back to your place,
have a chilled bottle of wine
or a warm pot of tea to share with each other.
Put on some easy listening music,
dim the lights,
and cuddle in front of the fireplace,
or take her out on the porch,
feel the breeze on your face,
or watch the sun set.
If you both get tired,
it may be time to take her home.
If you can't stand to see her leave you,
you may just go ahead
and grab her hand
and tell her why.
You may say "I love you."
"I won't let you leave my sight."

The night's over, and parties must part.
So here are the two definitive questions:
"Did you enjoy yourself?"
and
"Would you want to do this again sometime?"

Imaginations

What is the color of love?
How does anger smell?
When does happiness make you itch?
Who gives us the strength
    to get through each day?
Where can one taste a rainbow?
Why can't I touch the wind?
  ...Crazy questions for a school-boy.
The answers are neither right nor wrong.
They are captured in my imagination,
  and I must keep them from getting away.
I guard them against theft.
I hold them close to me so I won't lose them.

I can soar with the eagles
  or swim with the dolphins.
I can find a pot of gold at the end of the rainbow.
I can walk a mile, or a marathon,
  or just roll along in my chair.
I can jump high, scream loud, watch the sun set,
  or smell the cookies burning in the kitchen.
I can sail to the ends of the earth
  then grab a plane to return home.
Nothing can stop me,
  when my imagination runs riot.
Nothing can interfere with my journey
  while I'm hanging onto my imagination.
Nothing can keep me in this chair
  when I can close my eyes,
  and be anywhere I want to be....

Love is a sugary sweet rainbow
  high in the sky.
Anger smells like hot coals
  burning in the grill
Thick smoke grabbed by the wind
  caught as I run by.

God gives me the strength
  to get through each day.
And when happiness makes me itch,
  I scratch it!

My Fingers
Did the Talking

Before I could talk again
I would type my thoughts to people
as we would have a 'conversation'.
Others would ask me questions
with their voice,
and I would type my answers.
I didn't type very fast.
I only used one finger.
Sometimes people would not be
patient enough with me.
I would be in the middle of a thought,
and they would finish my thought for me.
I didn't like it when people finished my sentences;
because maybe they didn't know
exactly what I was thinking.

We saved my conversations on the computer.
When I look back now,
I see how disjointed they were.

The difference between
speaking words
and typing words is:
when the words come out of your mouth
you can add
expression: laughter, anger,
or any other emotion.
You can bring the words
from your heart.
Typing words in conversations
has not one bit of color to it.
There is no feeling, no spirit.
Sometimes I think people
don't take you as seriously,
when you're typing your thoughts or feelings
instead of speaking them.
Even when you're speaking about
how you feel,
they still may not be listening.

A Dream

What is a dream?
...a picture of the future;
...something one wants to happen,
       even though it may sound impossible;
...wishes and hopes;
...not always realistic, but one has the ability
       to make them a reality;
...once realized,
       the possibly that dreams may come true,
       one has the power to make them true;
...hard work will enable one's dreams
       to become authentic.

I have dreams like anyone else.
My dreams are exclusive to me.
I wish...
to be comfortable with my feelings about myself.
I hope...
to be accepting of my physical condition
at each stage of my rehabilitation.
I aspire...
to view my world with a positive attitude
and a positive self image.
I dream...
of getting out of this chair and walking again.

I have the vision...
of being independent,
taking care of myself;
taking care of my daily needs.
I want...
to be mobile, and also to drive again.
My ambition...
is to have a good job so I can live comfortably and not be dependent
on any other person.
I desire...
my own family, a wife and children.
And I pray...
to have friends who won't let me down nor go away without sharing
their leaving with me.

In order to realize my dreams,
  I must work hard to accept me
    as I am and as I change.
I will work hard...
  to keep my attitude positive.
I will work hard...
  to rehabilitate myself
    mentally and physically.
I will continue...
  to plan and dream; and dream and plan.
And one day...
  my dreams will become
    my reality.

My Cat

Sirus, my cat, with his bobbed tail
reminds me of a great, striped whale.
Out all night to hunt and stalk,
he sleeps all day just like a rock.

Doesn't care where he gets his pats,
as long as they come in a significant batch.
He loves to eat when he's awake,
not kitty food, but fish or steak.

Because his size is hefty,
often people approach him with worry.
But Sirus shows no hostility,
just friendliness and generosity.

Slithering along against those who come to call
he sheds his coat with no favoritism at all.
Pant legs, pillows, bed covers or chairs
leaving his signature without any airs.

With me he's quite at ease,
jumping on my lap, ready to please.
He purrs and squirms, resting on my knees.
Succor for him, comfort for me.

Once a stray, with no home to tie him,
now he's assured a family who loves him.
Happiness, contentment he shares with me;
I cherish the time spent in his company.

My Dog

Jake, my dog, is old and grey;
stays outside in the garage all day.
Mournfully baying as if at the full moon,
grunting at sounds, deaf to everyday tunes.

Jake is quite envious of Sirus, the cat,
who lies in the cooled house upon the mat.
While Jake is stuck out with the cars and bikes,
in rain, snow, or heat he does what he likes.

With his barrel shaped chest, and his lumbering pace,
he travels not far from his home, his 'base'.
He eats like a bear and he looks like one, too.
If you startle him, his thunderous bark may frighten you.

But Jake is sociable with all our friends,
scratch his ears or belly and he'll ask again.
Once you earn his favor, you'll remember the rule:
as his pal, you may be graced with his plentiful drool,

He's old and deaf and doesn't smell too good.
He goes for a bath, where he's pampered and loved.
He's worked hard as a guard for our family and home
now he paces a bit just as he roams.

Barking at sounds only he can hear,
he guards the house with his ancient manner.
Somber, aged, he likes sometimes to play,
but I think he's earned the right to sleep all day.

My Brother

Sometimes I judge him
and I'm not so kind.
I talk about his being irresponsible,
being loud, being stubborn,
not doing so well in school,
and some days
I would like to plunk him down
on a desert island
where he can't play his loud music
or his video games.
Or maybe he just wouldn't be born yet.

But he's my brother, Daniel,
younger by two years.
As young boys,
we got along pretty well.
We played basketball in the driveway
or tossed the baseball in the back yard.
In front of the TV, we used to play
those old Nintendo video games.
We attended church together.

As we grew into our teens our differences
became more and more pronounced
and we grew further apart.
These past couple of years
he's grown almost as tall as me.
His hair is now long
and his beard makes him look older
than his 17 years.
I still go to church, but he chooses not to.

He can be very funny
and make me laugh.
Not accepting help from anyone,
he struggles with his school work
but I know he tries as hard as he can.
He's good at sports; loves football.
When he comes home
covered with colors of paint,
I know he's been shooting
with some of his friends.
Those friends are mostly guys
who often stay at our house overnight.
I like it when he stays overnight with them
because it's quieter at home.
The walls vibrate with sounds of rap music
and loud expletives
as Daniel and his friends
shoot up the TV screen with his Xbox.
They play late into the night
and keep me awake.

I worry that he makes poor choices;
that he takes advice from the wrong people;
that he chooses the wrong friends.
I'm concerned for his future;
that he'll take the wrong path in life.
I pray he won't abuse his body or his mind.
I want him to succeed.
I love my brother, Daniel.

Fantasy

Today I sit and ponder
over the fantasies in my heart.
You could ask me "What is a fantasy?"

I define it as a vision of myself
in a place where something (like a dream)
may or may not occur;
where it might only be something
which would or wouldn't happen;
an idea I would only have
in my wildest imaginations.

Some fantasies are silly:
Because my younger brother drives me crazy,
I fantasize about dropping him
onto a deserted island
with no access to his video games system!

I also have some heartfelt fantasies :
I think about being normal again:
getting back all of my former physical capabilities
and a healthy state of mind.
I close my eyes and I see
a life with a wife and three kids.
I visualize my life in a hospital
helping others in the medical profession.
I see myself surrounded by good friends,
who stay close and support me.

Are these fantasies?
Can I believe that one day they will come true?

movement

planets circling around the sun
feet peddling two wheels down an open lane
the wind gusting through the trees
memories illusively skimming across the mind
fish gliding in the water
baseball soaring over the heads of little leaguers
hands rotating on the face of a clock
birds swooping to the feeder at the window
dogs galloping across an open field
legs scissoring through the blue coolness of a pool
deer gracefully bounding through the woods
airplanes lifting their wings thrusting into the sky
toddlers waddling to a mother's grasp
a blender's blades whirling its contents; pirouetting
a finger typing unhurriedly on the keyboard
waves undulating on the horizon
automobiles at high speed on a dark country road
blood pumping and pulsing though the body
parents crying; friends despairing; praying, praying
years passing; comatose to aware; unconscious to alert
wheels turning assisting me to getting around
feet taking one step at a time; learning to walk again

movement

a dream come true

Summertime

Heat…sunny warm days and nights
    catching a breeze as it scampers by
    sprinting through the sprinkler to cool off
    cool ice cream trickling down your throat
    air conditioning inside
        when the outside is unbearable

Doings…catching 'the big one' in the shady fishing hole
    jumping into the cool blue water of a pool
    sailing on crystal clear lake water
    grilling hot dogs over a barbeque fire
    camping out under the summer stars
    vacations to sunny beaches
        or cool mountain vistas

Games…hitting a homerun for the home team
    kicking a goal with dreams of the World Cup
    volley and slice the ball across the net
    stroking, reaching out to part the cool water

Growth…soft rain helping corn fields grow
    high as an elephant's eye
    vegetable gardens lush with colorful bounty
    farmers tending and reaping
    the scent of onions and freshly mowed grass
    shades of green abound
    flowers of varied hue and scent
        blossom everywhere

Kids…summer break from school
    tanning in the summer sun
    sandals and flip flops, relaxing in the heat
    shorts and tank tops, skin glowing
    flat tops and bobs, with solar highlights
    running in the freedom of summertime

Romance

I close my eyes and think of romance.

What do you think about
        when you think of romance?
    ...chocolate covered cherries?
    ...a gift of jewelry?
    ...going to a play or a musical?
    ...making a tuna sandwich,
    ...sharing a bottle of white wine late at night?
    ...watching a romantic movie together?
    ...red roses and a candlelight dinner?

What about a romantic getaway, a cruise
        to an exotic city or locale?
I imagine lying on a beach in the sun,
        my love beside me.
We could take a walk on the beach,
        holding hands
        while watching the sun set.

How about a trip to the Azores,
        a most beautiful island location?
I can see spending the night together
        under a palm tree
        gazing at the glorious moon and stars
        as they move across the sky.
Finally, both tired but you don't want to sleep,
        afraid of missing something exciting.

I close my eyes and think of romance...

Independence Defined

B.C. – Before the Crash
I remember
    I had another life; an independent life.
I remember
    coming and going
    whenever and wherever I wanted.
I remember
    running to the neighbor's house or to my friends'.
I remember
    playing baseball and swimming.
I remember
    going to the mall or my favorite store, "Borders".
I remember
    working on the computer or doing mechanical stuff
    around the house.
I remember
    earning money
    while umpiring little league baseball games
    in the spring.
I remember
    having friends overnight or
    going to their homes to play or hang out.
I remember
    being at that point where I was beginning
    to handle relationships with girls on my own.
I remember
    doing things by myself: cooking a bit, cleaning my room,
    taking a shower.
I remember
    getting my license and driving the car.

A.C. – After the Crash
They tell me
    I was driving and hit a tree;
    My independence was lost.
They tell me

I lay in bed, comatose for a long while.
They tell me
    I was not moving.
They tell me
    I was hooked to all sorts of machines,
    beeping and pulsing all day and all night long.
They tell me
    I had strangers moving me, touching me,
    prodding me, giving me medication
    with a needle.
They tell me
    I was hooked to iv's and machines;
    machines to help me breathe
    and my heart to keep on beating.
They tell me
    I had a severe head injury.
They tell me
    I would never walk again.
They tell me
    that they all worried about
    and prayed for me.

H.C. - Home Coming

I remember
    returning to my own room,
    becoming dependent on parents once again.
I remember
    visiting nurses who cleaned me and changed the beddings.
I remember
    awareness of my life
    returning to me gradually.
I remember
    first moving my arm, then moving my leg;
    feeling pins and needles all through my body,
    as my nervous system once again
    began to function.
I remember
    being pushed in a wheelchair

to get me out of my room for a while.
I remember
    sitting in my wheelchair
    and watching movies on the TV.
I remember
    my parents taking me to physical therapy.
I remember
    pointing to pictures to communicate
    with my home teacher.
I remember
    using the computer's keyboard in lieu of voice
    to talk with my family and friends.
I remember
    beginning to use my voice again;
    then the 'trache' coming out.
I remember
    getting the electric chair;
    moving about the house on my own.

I remember
    returning to school;
    finding success in my classes.
I remember
    first steps, once again;
    as I begin to relearn to walk.

A.D. – Again inDependent
I tell them
    I've got the dedication
    to walk independently again.
I tell them
    I will graduate from high school.
I tell them
    I will regain my normal life.
I tell them
    I remember Independence.
    And now I can see it
    once again returning to me.

Father
(a Prayer)

Father,

I thank you for the gift of your Son, Christ Jesus,
Who came to this earth to be crucified and die
so that our sins could be forgiven.
And I thank You for the gift of life
that has been given to me.
I am looking forward to fulfilling the promise
that my faith offers:
that I will spend eternity with You in Your house.

Help me to get through the rougher parts of my life:
disappointing times, loss of family members, or
daily struggles with emotions or physical pain.
Help me to comprehend the design you have for me
and the ability to acknowledge your plan.

Please give me comfort as I wrestle with depression.
Comfort me daily and help heal my impurities;
especially the helplessness I feel
with my limited physical capabilities.

For others in my life, I ask for their acceptance of me.
Bring back to me the friendships I've lost
since my accident.
Help others see my reality and
understand the confusion I sometimes have.
Give your comfort and love to those
whose lives are broken or in struggle.
Help them to see the light of hope as I do
through Your Son.

All this I ask, in Jesus' name….Amen.

Friendship

A friend is someone
      who might cheer you up if you're blue
or a person to share your happiness
      if you're in a good mood.
There is comfort in knowing that with a friend,
      there is always somewhere for you to go,
or someone who will come visit you
      when she wants to be together.
If you need help you can go to your friend,
      or just hang out if there's nothing to do.
A friend is a person who will always be supportive of you
      or stay connected if they're away,
      providing you with unbroken assurance .
A friend will listen to you when you need to vent,
      or will be quiet when you need solitude.
A friend will walk you through
      the difficult circumstances in your life
and share the positive ones
      as they come along.
You can share ideas or feelings with her
      that you might not share with anyone else
or she will respect your privacy
      if you choose not to share.
It's someone you can trust
      and who trusts you.
A person with whom you have lots in common,
      or you compliment each other
      is a friend with whom you "fit".
A friend will accept you for what you are
      and will be able to accept any
      changes you may have in your life
or at least accept the fact that change has occurred
      and be able to deal with it.
A true friend will be your friend for life.
      Everybody needs a friend.

Memories

What happens to our brains
when a memory becomes a reality?
Or when the events we remember as happening
are challenged by others who say
that they never occurred?
Some things I remember with clarity.
They are meaningful to me, my family, and my friends.
Some incidents, they say, I'm *not* remembering correctly.
They tell me that I am imagining pieces of my past.
But who is better to know my real memories than myself?
They say I am remembering things that haven't happened yet.
I question: how can that be?
Are my family and friends telling me stories?
Or are my own memories playing tricks on me?
Some days I think I am right.
Other days I'm beginning to believe it IS my memory
that's trying to deceive me.
But how can you stop trusting yourself,
when that would be stopping
one of the very things that makes you human?
Many of the people in my life tell me
my memories are incorrect.
They challenge me with questions about 'their' realities.
Could I be losing my mind?
The scariest part of this is that there's nothing I can do
to prove that my memories are true.
But "I" believe my memories are accurate,
and that's all that matters.
I remember them.
I believe that they are my true past.
The key issue about "past" is that it's over
so therefore it must have already happened.
These memories will remain with me for all eternity.

Reflections on Goal-setting

Do you choose your goals,
                or do your goals choose you?
Setting goals in our lives helps us
                to improve ourselves.
We pick goals that are achievable;
                ones that we will likely be able to reach.
We need to feel success and not frustration.
Why pick a goal if you cannot achieve it?
                If you do then you've already lost.
So you begin by picking something in your life
                that you want to change or improve.
Write down your goal as if you've already achieved it.
Now it has become a positive statement for you.
Then list the ways you might be able to achieve that goal.
Choose the ones that might be suitable for you,
                be reasonable to accomplish
                and set up objectives to reach that goal.
How hard are you willing to work to reach that goal?
What obstacles might get in your way
                and how can you bypass them?
As you work through your list of objectives,
                your goal will be coming closer to being fulfilled.
As you near your goal, you may find that you think better
                of yourself for your perseverance.
As you perfect your goal,
                you find a deep sense of satisfaction
                        growing inside of you.
This satisfaction accompanies the perfection of the goal.
Perfection is now defined as your goal being achieved.
                Now it's time to start on another goal.

Complete

Before we met I didn't felt whole.
Once I met you
my outlook on life became more positive.
This perspective was a change for the better.
Now every time you go away
those feelings of incompleteness return.
So if it wouldn't be asking too much,
could we please at least stay in touch?
It would help me dramatically
to keep my life in a positive perspective.
Could we continue to at least be friends?
You know? I'd love our friendship to grow
into a more complex relationship.
I don't feel I can live a full nor complete life without you.
I can't stand being apart from you.
Would you please search your heart,
and consider coming back into my life?
I am weary of allowing myself to get too close to someone
and not have those feelings returned.
My answer to this problem?
"Stay away from members of the opposite sex,"
These days, I try to steer clear of relationships.
And I won't allow my feelings to exceed the level of
'friendship'; although for me it doesn't seem to be possible.
Controlling the intensity within my relationships
isn't as easy as it sounds
I seem to be lost without you.
Please consider coming back to me
so I may once again feel complete.
I am not happy living without you,
therefore you complete me.

Movies

Alone in the room,
I find electronic camaraderie
in the form of the TV remote;
no one with whom to compete for the control.
One touch of a button
brings the colorful world of movies to my fingertips.
My choices are almost infinite:
a movie to make me laugh and brighten my day;
a movie to make me cry,
        to awaken emotions safely hidden deep within;
a who-done-it to make me think
        and challenge my creativity;
        one to frighten me into the safety of my couch;
or a love story to warm my heart
        and allow me to recall relationships past
        or rekindle hopes of those to come.
I can sing along with an opera's light aria
        or join a popular artist in a musical comedy,
        with no household critics
        to insinuate that I belong at the local dog pound.
Movies take me away from daily chores or worries.
Movies can open doors to foreign cities,
        fly me to faraway fantasy lands
        or show me life just outside my back yard.
I can relive history
or catch a glimpse into some director's concept of the future.
A movie that is remade from a book
        gives me an opportunity to compare the two
        and judge which I prefer.
No matter what, movies open new vistas to me
        and offer me choices
to escape for just a while out of my everyday world.

THE CHAIR

There is life before "the chair"
        and life after "the chair".
Two lives....separate yet the same.....
Before the chair, there was:
        swimming,   running,
strolling,   jumping,
        walking into a restaurant anonymously,
friends all around,
        friends, not embarrassed to be seen with me,
living room football games with my brother
           when my parents were away,
family outings,   camping,   to the local park,
      dating,   driving to restaurants,
         dancing,
            Salsa,   Merengue.
Then came "the chair"....
A gift!   A curse!   A gifted curse!
After the chair, friendships diminish.
There are pitiful stares from strangers.
There is distance and unease between brothers.
There is 'mobility,'
        'handicapped accessible' rooms,
bathrooms,   hotel rooms,   houses,   churches...
        dependence on others for basic needs.
After the chair, there is loneliness and being alone.
There is measured progress in independence.
After the chair, strangers come into my life
        and become treasured friends;
people I would never have met were it not for 'the chair'.
After the chair, life is different. Life is changed.
And when something bad happens to put you in a chair,
you get a glimpse of how precious and valuable life is.

Back To School

Bells ringing...
Waves of teenage bodies exiting yellow buses
where drivers have worked to entertain and maintain
sanity among the crowds...
Hallways crammed with jeans & t's,
khaki & cotton, jocks & geeks & goth & BLING...
Voices combining to create a cacophony of noise...
School is back in session.
Getting up early only to race to class
to challenge the teacher with ideas, opinions and attitude.
Struggling with lockers...Managing books and notebooks...
Praying for that study hall to complete unfinished work.
Lunchroom antics, where the food is decent
and the atmosphere is frantic.
Who is funnier, the kids acting goofy
or the lunch ladies with their comic banter to lighten your day?
Gym glass is over; time to change;
chatting with some friends in the locker room with only a smidgen of time
till the bell rings;
now you're faced with the most frantic question:
to be or not to be...tardy!
A call to the office...late to class? ...missing work?
 ...smoking in the boys room? ...or just a change in schedule?
Teachers, the heroes of the present...
making jokes while trying to infuse into their students
a love of learning and a quest to improve and mature.
Friends who crack wise in the halls, rushing to class;
maybe an argument, confrontation and resolution...
Friends who keep you together;
who become your pals or your dates for Friday night.
Challenges and frustrations...class discussions, homework,
growing up, relationships with girls.
Sports competitions, dances, science fairs, art shows, music
concerts and plays...always something to do or
somewhere to go.
The final bell to signal the end of a challenging day.
Each day the same; a mix of emotions, laughter,
sometimes tears and hard work.

Dreams

I have dreams.
Don't you?
I dream of being able to do everything
that I want to do,
both mentally and physically.
I dream of being accepted by others,
and not to be thought of or even viewed
as an outcast because of this chair.
I dream of having no confusion
about life's capabilities…
just clear thinking each and every day.
Dreams are similar to fantasies,
although dreams seem more likely
to come true.
I guess it depends on how much
you want it to become true.
Always keep your dreams alive.
Choose a dream that you want to fulfill.
Work on a plan to make it true.
Stay focused.
And your dream will become a reality.
I think dreams are meant to come true. Don't you?

Halloween

Happy faces! Scary faces!
Walking around to different places!
Dress up, children! Costumes and masks!
"Trick or Treat?" A question asked.
Travel about from house to house!
There's a cat! There's a mouse!
Dark streets, full moon and owls that hoot!
Parents join kids collecting their loot!
Running around from place to place!
Enjoying the night with a smiling face!

Show off your costume! Treats for all!
Go 'round your neighborhood or the local mall!
Candy in your bags! Tricks and treats!
Supermen, wizards or ghosts in sheets!
Parties and contests with prizes for the best!
Funniest? Scariest? Not one looks like the rest!

Later teens go out to parties!
Dressed as hobos, superfreaks or Smarties!
Who's the box of cereal over there?
Salt and pepper shakers or a big can of beer!
Going through houses, haunted and dark!
Just brave teens, out for a lark!

Grown-ups, too, enjoy the day
With parties, bonfires and rides in the hay.
Kings or queens, or vampires scary!
Who's that monster, big and hairy!
Youngsters, oldsters, and in between,
there's something for everyone at Halloween!

Death

What is death but a natural step in life?
"We are born. We live. We die".
We watch it happening in nature from day to day.
Flowers begin as seeds,
      grow to bloom and
           then close their leaves and die.
We see it with 'things' in our lives:
      clocks, washing machines,
           televisions, any 'thing' you may find.
They work for a while,
      and then they don't.
Babies are born.
      Children grow up.
           Adults mature.
                The elderly pass away.
Death sometimes may come earlier than expected.
We never know when death may take us from this life.
We question why a child is taken from our lives in illness
      or a young adult on an instant's notice in a car accident,
           or a young mother as she births her child.
Sometimes we don't die but live on,
      like a living death.
Oh, the sadness this brings to a family
      when their loved one is only living because of machines.
We shouldn't be afraid of the big D word, "death"!
We ought not look at death with a negative eye.
      We'll pass from this earthly world.
           Our family and friends will miss us.
But, we will finally get to meet our One True Heavenly Father, "God".
We'll be in a much better place.
So don't be afraid of the big bad D word
      or look at it with the wrong point of view.
           Death is just a normal part of life.
                Put your heart at peace.

CHOICES

Our walk through life is all about making choices.
Some choices you make on an instant's notice.
Some choices you may have the time
to think about: for a little bit, a few seconds,
a minute, an hour, a week, a day,
or maybe even longer.

Choices that take you down
the major highways in life
could be 'life changing':
After high school do you attend college
or run straight into the workforce?
What major field of study will you pursue?
With whom will you fall in love
and eventually marry ?
Will you begin a family right away
or wait a few years?
What house or brand of car will you purchase?
If problems arise in your marriage,
do you remain married or become divorced?
Which job offer do you accept?
Will it take you from your home to places unknown?

The personal choices you make
effect the path on which you walk in life:
Do you choose kindness or selfishness?
Can you handle your anger issues,
or do they eat you alive?
Do you know how to deal with problems
or do you blow things way out of proportion
and react?
How much or how little do you eat?
Will you or won't you exercise?
Do you go to bed early or
do you stay up late as a night owl"?

Do you work hard or take it easy?
Do you cut classes or attend regularly?
Do you choose drugs and alcohol,
or do you stay sober?
Can you live without cigarettes
or are you hooked?
Can you choose among your acquaintances
who will become your friends?
Do you attend church each week,
believe what you're taught there,
or do you stay home, alone?
Do you let go and let God help
or do you handle life's problems all by yourself?

With your everyday choices,
it's like taking a stroll.
You can either walk along with everyone else
or take a sprint down that narrow path:
Do you have that second cup of coffee or those extra cookies?
Do you choose to either wake up early
or to stay asleep?
Will you jog to school or take a leisurely walk?
Do you or don't you choose to do your homework?
Can you stay home or go out with the guys every Friday night?

We do have to remember that
all choices have consequences.
When you make a choice you have to be prepared
to accept the consequences for your actions.
Making good choices in life
isn't as easy as it sounds.
Therefore be careful of the choices you make
as you walk the path of your life.

Thoughts on Leadership
By Michael Grego
(Written for Dr. H .Douglas Williams, Superintendent of MSD Perry Township)

There are leaders, and there are good leaders.
A good leader is someone who is strong;
A person you could go to in time of need;
Someone who will walk you through complicated times;
Who supports you in disappointing circumstances.
A good leader may not appear to be your friend,
When decisions he makes
seem to not be in your interest.
But he could be a friend when you need one.
He is experienced in life,
And, even though you may not be able to keep from worrying,
He can help you get through a tight spot,
Because he's 'been there'!
A good leader will organize and departmentalize.
He will distribute jobs with his eye on each one.
He will give credit when it's due
And call you on a mistake if it's necessary.
He will teach you.
He will guide you.
He can be judge and jury.
But he will be fair.
He is goal centered
And expects you to be also.

Thanks for being a good leader to our schools.

Focus

A thought.
It grows.
Concentrate.
Be singular in your thought.
Bring it to life.
Don't become distracted.
Attend to the task.
Baby steps.
Don't ask for help.
Absorb yourself in the task.
Don't give up.
Stay positive.
Be vigilant.
Deliberate.
Center.
Be fastidious.
Build your vision,
One step at a time.

Opinions

Many people will tell you
to keep your opinions to yourself.
I wonder why that is?
Opinions belong to the individual.
Opinions have to do with feelings.
Opinions are quite personal.
Opinions can be constructive,
pessimistic or even mediocre.
Sometimes offering an opinion to another
may be overstepping your bounds.
Sometimes keeping your opinion inside
might really trouble you
if you don't communicate it to another.

Facts are statements of truth.
Facts can be proven by observation.
Facts are reality.
Facts generally have no right or wrong.
They are just facts.

Can you compare facts and opinions?
You can compare them,
but remember they are quite different.
Two people could have
two very different opinions
about any subject
even though they are talking
about the same thing.

The difference between an opinion
and a fact is that
facts can be proven and
opinions are what you think or feel
about a subject.

You may give your opinion when asked
in any situation.
It may be helpful or harmful,
enthusiastic or disapproving.
There is no correct answer with an opinion.

People who ask for opinions
may not really want to hear yours.
So be wary of what you offer.
Be careful you do not insult
or hurt another's feelings.
If your opinions aren't meant
for a helpful purpose,
then it's better for you
to keep your opinions to yourself.

A Crush

Ah, youth!
Attraction…
Secretive and warm!
A flush of anticipation,
Excitement…
Beyond friendship!
When did the feelings change?
How did the feelings change?
Why did the feelings change?
Obsessive thoughts!
Infatuated…
A search for attention,
Willing to do anything!
Foolish or romantic…
Sometimes shy!
Sometimes not!
Delighting in the heat!
Reveling in the exhilaration!
A crush!
(one of the seven deadly sins?)

The Teacher

Varied personalities and backgrounds
walk into the classroom and sit before her.
She empowers each with skills
to survive and be successful.
She attempts to meet their needs.
Guidance and advice is offered freely;
As is encouragement and support,
    honesty and fairness.
Dealing with the moods of teens
or the hungry belly of a little one;
Offering a challenge;
Arguing a point;
she teaches reason,
    perseverance,
        and cooperation
to self involved youth.
Steering them toward the right path,
she keeps them moving
    should they hit a bump in the road.
They ought to give back respect and gratitude,
but often not.
It's sometimes a thankless job.
More often it's a job that offers
many thankful
    and promising moments.

My Thoughts on Confidence

I could give you MY definition of having confidence:
You can accomplish anything you set your mind to,
no matter how difficult it is!
That can include homework, projects such as the science fair,
sports, relationships or a job.
You can work through any hardships
that life seems to throw in your way.
But you have to *believe* you can make it
through life with or without its troubles.
As for going to school, you might not see the positives
as you're going through.
Although later, you'll figure out that it's all for the good,
for jobs and/or goals you may set for yourself in the future.

Before my accident I had a positive attitude towards my life
with no exceptions.
I used to play sports (track, cross country, soccer, swimming, baseball).
I also used to play the alto sax in the school band.
I went to all my classes and didn't have to struggle for good grades.
I'd be persistent with a class or subject,
keep on working, until I was done;
satisfied or happy with my performance.
I felt secure enough that I could work in a quick and a doubtless manner in
my actions.
I believed I was respected by all of my friends
who were from a wide range of people.
I was sort of a mix between a 'band geek', a 'jock' and a 'nerd'.
It never bothered me to be known as being from any of those groups.
I felt that it was good there was a piece of me in each of those groups.
It introduced me to a whole lot of different people from varied backgrounds.
I thought that as a jock, I wouldn't have as many good friends.
Or maybe jocks seemed to be more of a clique to me.
They sort of stuck with themselves, or with other jocks.
I wasn't like that.
I'd learned to stay away from becoming too much of a part of any one group.
I knew I wanted more.
That is why I became a 'mix'.
I believe my popularity went down a bit but I found my best friend,
a "flute player" named Tiffany.
The kids in the band were friendly and out going.
And I was looking for friends that would stay with me for life.

My confidence dropped a few notches after my accident.
To put it more realistically my confidence went into the gutter.
At first, I'd lost all my physical and mental capabilities.
Now I'm stuck in this dog-gone wheelchair.
My attitude is improving as I gain back some of my lost abilities,
although it's not like it used to be.
My perseverance level has greatly diminished.
Before the accident I'd work on anything with no hesitation
or second thought.
Now I must be greatly interested on a certain topic
in order for me to get the determination to work on it.
Anger began knocking at my door
although I'm not really planning on letting it in.
I'm not as sure of what I'm doing nor my next step.
I don't remember things as well as I used to.
I sometimes feel like no one respects me anymore.
My friends moved on in with their lives and I feel 'stuck' in mine.
Some of my former friends are in college and some are just gone.
One day I hope to catch up with them.
And then some days, I don't understand why I have no friends.
And now it's back to school to finish what I began.
I don't like going, but I understand I must.
I'm not planning on giving up anytime soon.
Because I can't move around on my own, come and go,
I am now limited in my choices of what I can or can't do in my own life.
I can't control where I go or what I do.
I can only go where this chair lets me go.
I need help with even simple daily tasks.
I feel like I lost my freedom.

Inside of me I haven't changed much.
The outside of me has changed and people don't see the confident man I am.
Therefore, often, 'I' don't see the confident man I used to be.
I work hard to make myself better.
I want to recapture that level of confidence I used to have
so I can do anything that I put my mind to doing.

health

good health
a state of well being
body and mind working perfectly
without complaint or problem
doctors inform
self education is paramount
health questions?
simple issues:
colds, fever, allergies, or broken bones;
complex health problems:
degenerative or life threatening
hodgkin's or muscular dystrophy,
a heart attack, or cancer;
problems at birth:
cerebral palsy, epilepsy, or spinal-bifida.
problems of old age:
dementia, or hardening of the arteries

good health -> accident -> wheelchair
unexpected
health prospects changed
drastic! immediate!
physical limitations improve daily
illness easier to come by

ultimate want: perfect health
needless worry
accidents -> out of the ordinary
always a solution
sickness getting in the way?
barring accomplishments?
adversity or illness?
stay positive
seek help
fight

The Rose

To me the rose is a symbol of love and caring,
Offered as a sign of friendship and sharing;
Humble suitor to sweet young maiden,
A joyful gift on a special occasion.

Innocence and purity, the white rose blooms,
At the start of a relationship or for one that's groomed.
Caution, for it also asks for secrecy or silence,
Or reverence to a partner, a humble alliance.

Shades of pink, varieties blossom
A graceful 'thank you' or to tell her she's awesome.
Light pink offers sympathy or admiration.
Dark pink demonstrates gratitude or appreciation.

When in need of a promise, a new beginning
The yellow rose gives you voice.
In joy, gladness or delight in friendship
The yellow rose makes a good choice.

When desire is overwhelming
And spirits need a lift,
Enthusiasm is difficult to curb
Offer the orange rose as a gift.

Often given to a lover,
Or to reveal respect for another,
Or offered to a knight who lays bare his courageousness
The red rose may also declare her beauty and gracefulness.

Blend red with white
Given the opportunity,
Indicating to her
You are 'one', in unity.

Rosebuds, so delicate in their presentation,
Purity and loveliness, the red's dedication.
A symbol of youth or girlhood: the chaste white;
The thorn less rose tells of the joy of 'love at first sight'.

Choose wisely the rose you send,
For lover, partner, sympathy or friend.

Who Is Your Friend?

...the person who makes you smile,
    or helps you think for a while;
...who might just make you cry,
    or cause you to sometimes ask "why?";
...the person on whose help you can count,
    for that homework assignment
        or that picture to mount;
...who supports you through good times or bad;
...who won't disappoint you or act like a cad;
...someone who'll point out
    if you're acting the fool;
...who won't put you down
    and thinks you are cool;
...someone you can trust,
    and if things fall apart
    helps put you back together,
    leads from the heart.
...a person with whom you can work or play,
    will get in trouble with you
    and laugh all the way;
...somebody who is honest and true;
    whose face mirrors your feelings
    happy or blue;
...a person who knows when you're lonely
    or smug
    and who'll leave you alone or
    give you a hug?
Who is your friend? Have you many or few?
Count them.
    Appreciate them
    ...the old and the new.

Recovery

Working hard from day to day
Pushing the limits all the way
To return to the life that I preferred
before the accident had occurred.
Never giving up till I meet my goals
of regaining independence, being whole.
To control my body the way it's designed
Attempting skills once known, now left behind
Regaining control of my body's symmetry
Relearning to walk, strengthening abilities.
Maintaining a positive mind set: I CAN!
Doing anything and everything so I will walk again.

Not wanting to be out of the ordinary,
Nor different from everyone else;
Not being gawked at or thought of in any different way
Not being treated as an outcast or in the way.
Not being considered handicapped or disabled;
But to be accepted as one who is capable.

I won't stop until it is done
Lots of work till 'the race is run'.
Therapists, ministers, teachers and friends
Helping, supporting me till the end.
Parents and family, loving and working
With church members, youth groups, classmates, all serving;
Gaining strength each day toward recovery
Managing feelings, the heart's discovery
Helps me as the journey unfolds
Slowly the progress towards all of my goals.

A Prayer for Help

Lord,
I praise You for Your Glory
While at Christmas I hear Your story
Of beginning life like me as a Babe
And then hearing of those You saved.
I ask you bless me with Your love
Look down on me from above
As I go through trying times
Please be with me, by my side.
Allow me to ask for help from You
To keep me sane as I go through
Disappointments in life that upset me
Give me the strength to see
Your assistance in my life
As I struggle with turmoil and strife.
Thank You for always being there for me
In Jesus' name I ask of Thee.

Thoughts on Appreciation

Appreciation...thankfulness, gratitude, indebtedness...
We thank God for His ultimate gift of life.
We appreciate our parents for our homes and the love they share with us
from day to day.
We value our friends and our loved ones.
We are thankful for others' generosity and hospitality towards us.
We are pleased with the 'things' we are able to accumulate in our lives.
We recognize the value of our health, living conditions, family, friends, and
money.
We are grateful for the rights we have as citizens in our own country.
We appreciate the troops who fight for our freedom and maintain our
country's freedom and peace.
There are so many things for which we can be thankful.
I am thankful for all the circumstances I've mentioned.
But, I have a few other things for which I am appreciative.
I am alive, when I could have died.
I am conscious when I could have remained in a comatose state.
I can speak when I might never have regained that ability
                    (and now there's no shutting me up!).
I can now read and write when I thought I'd lost those skills for good.
I am walking once again, when I thought I'd be stuck in this chair forever.
I've a long way to go, but I appreciate all that I've accomplished so much, so
far.
I appreciate the help I've received from so many different sources.
I appreciate each day I can wake up and begin a new day.
And because I can wake up and start a new day again, I appreciate
everything with which God has blessed me from head to toe!

Courtesy

Courtesy has become a forgotten art;
One which we need to revive.
Saying, "I'm sorry" or "Thank you";
Greeting someone when they arrive;

Shaking their hand, while saying "Hello";
"Nice to see you again." or saying "Good-bye";
Holding open a door for another: "ladies first";
Offering your bus seat to one less spry;

Picking up after your-self at home;
Not littering out in the street;
Letting another car ahead of you
at the stop sign;
Letting someone in front of you
when buying puffed wheat.

The gift of courtesy is free to all.
You just have to remember
To use your manners every day
"January through December".

Thoughts on Envy

Everybody wants to improve their lives.
We all want or dream of a nicer house,
finer cars,
more fashionable clothing,
better jobs,
or a higher income.
There is a big difference between
wanting and envying.
Envy leads to greed and sometimes
resentment or spite.
Some people are envious of other's money,
income, health or physical appearance.
People can also become envious
of other people's 'things' or material possessions.
Often when the envied object is obtained,
then there is bragging and
further wanting which,
more often than not,
leads to greed.
A greedy person may resent what others have.
He may become spiteful
if he cannot have what he wants.
He may become demanding in his envy or greed.
The greedy person either stays covetous
or he has to want to change;
be less materialistic.
Envy does not improve one's life
but only complicates it.
Envy can eat at one's heart
in addition to altering his life.
There is nothing wrong with
wanting to improve your lot in life,
but improvements ought to occur
when your income allows you to live
in a more affluent way.
Then you can live the life of which you dreamed.

More Thoughts on Appreciation

Feelings of gratitude or thanks
often forgotten, sometimes not quite enough;
...to anyone who would help you through a hard,
   disappointing, or difficult time;
...to your parents who love you and assist you
   through each life task,
...for the meals being put on the table regularly,
...for the warm, hospitable home they've created for you,
...for their guidance as you mature and become independent;
...to friends because they stand beside you with
   their support and encouragement;
...to the teachers who help you grow in knowledge
   and wisdom;
...to coaches who give confidence and promote
   healthy competition;
...to the doctors and nurses who keep us healthy;
...to the police and firefighters who maintain our
   peace and safety;
...to our Father in heaven for the gift of life;
...for each and every beautiful, wonderful, and glorious day
...for making sure you stay on the right path and
   remain in perfect health.
As for me, I appreciate the opportunity to thank my
family and friends for all the help I received following
my car accident:
...for my parents unending support and love;
...for the friends who visited and their caring;
...for the therapists and teachers who stuck by me
   and helped me gain back the skills I've lost;
...for the church members who prayed for me and
   were by my side through everything;
...for accepting me for whom I am and
   who I am becoming;
...for the support I receive through each stage
   of my recovery.

Emotion

Emotion shapes our day-to-day lives:
The feeling of happiness or disappointment,
The sentiment of love or affection,
The sensation of exhilaration or fear,
The passion of intimacy or drive.
Meet a new friend, or renew an old friendship
                    and you feel gladness.
Lose a friend and disappointment or sadness sets in.
Feel the softness of a kitten's coat
                    and experience a child-like joy.
Enjoy the companionship of a dog for many years
            and feel the safety and camaraderie he offers.
Get a good grade in school and feel pride.
Fired from a job opens the door to despair.
Offer your love to another
            and experience an array of feelings,
            ranging from hot passion,
                    to warm comfort,
                        to lighthearted happiness,
                            to relaxed contentment.
Ride on a roller coaster
and your emotions follow you up the highest peaks,
dive into breathtaking valleys
            only to climb back up
                    as the fear, delight and excitement
                        continue to chase you.
Sit quietly on a deserted beach, feel the breeze
            blowing on your face
                    and sense soft pleasure.
Bury a loved one
            and the pain and grief can be overwhelming.
Witness the birth of a baby
            and feel the caress of awe-inspiring wonder.
Sit in a quiet church
            and be touched with the peace
                    and love of God.

PRIDE

Arrogance
Forward   Overconfident
Lording   Self-asserting   Advancing
Conceit   Pride   Modesty   Humbleness
Crushing   Unassuming   Trusting
Meek   Gratified
Humility

SHINE

Bright light shines on me
Frightens away the darkness
Heart opens for love

STRENGTH

Tall oak with jade leaves
Majestic ruling wonder
She humbles my soul

SURVIVAL

Reckless wind rends rips
Bitter cold or blazing sun
Still she stands stalwart

A Prayer For Accomplishment

Lord,
Each day I wake.
Each day I thank You
for the gifts I have received.
I pray that I will honor You
with my actions this day.
Give me the grace to be kind today.
Give me the patience
to tolerate intolerance.
Be by my side as I work and play.
Help me to love others as You love me.
Support me when I need a hand.
Encourage me when I feel in need.
I will do my best
to make You proud of me today.
And, Father, I pray
You will be waiting with open arms
Saying, "Good job son."

More Thoughts on Confidence

Don't allow anything to stop you from completing your task,
whether it is an essay for school,
        a popularity issue or a project at work.
Believe in yourself.
     Set a goal and stick to it.
Make sure your goals are achievable.
By meeting simple goals
     you will develop self-assurance in your abilities.
Add a few challenging goals to inspire you to improve yourself.
You may need to develop some confidence
        when trying to do something new:
        a sport, a dance,
        playing a musical instrument, or
        traveling to unknown destinations.
If you have a self-assured friend by your side
you may be able to glean some of that confidence from him.
When people see you as a self-reliant, poised person,
     they know that you are confident.
Being able to live with your convictions with certainty
     also reflects an air of confidence.
That coolness you exude will benefit your schooling,
        your work, and your life experiences.

Cherish

How can I tell you
how much I cherish you?
Can I explain the pleasure I feel
when you enter the room?
The warmth envelopes me
like a cloak on a dismal day.
There's not a way in heaven or on earth
to share the vastness of my feelings.
You're so incredibly valuable.
Nothing upon this earth
could possibly please me
any more than keeping our relationship
as vital as it was when we first met.
Do you remember?
You were standing across the room
at a school dance.
When I saw you,
you took my breath away.
Your hair shined like the sunlight.
I didn't think my feet
would carry me over to you.
And then when I finally approached you,
your smile dazzled me
as you took my hand
and we walked onto the dance floor.
I've not wanted to let you out of my arms since then.
How blessed I have been
to have you as part of my life.

Purity

newly fallen snow
the fresh smell of rain
a tripping forest stream
an honorable act of kindness.
the smell of baking cookies.
a cascading waterfall
purple crocuses as they peek out of the spring soil
a baby's laughter
angelic clouds in a bright blue sky
a refreshing cup of ice cold water on a hot humid day
a mother's milk
fresh country air
the innocence of a child
a babbling brook in the quiet of the woods
the soft touch of a baby's skin
crashing ocean waves on a white hot beach
a mother's love
the sinless Christ

About The Author

Hello, I am Michael. I was born in Indianapolis, Indiana on January 28, 1987. My mother's family name is Paul, and my father's family name is Grego. Therefore my last name is Grego. I have one younger brother, Daniel. I have an old black lab named Jake and a large bob cat named Sirus. I went to Franklin Central High School where I was active in sports (baseball, swimming, cross country, soccer) and band (I played the alto sax.) Then on June 13, 2003, I was in a car accident and all of a sudden "in one fell swoop" everything familiar to me was taken from me. I only know a few things about my accident. I was told that I was coming home from a friend's party when I lost control of the Cavalier I was driving. I lost control of the car and ran head on into a park fence and a tree. And 'no' I wasn't drunk but I may have been going a bit too fast. Being a relatively new driver when I hit a bump I lost control of the car. Later I found myself at the hospital in a comatose state. I have what is called Traumatic Brain Injury. I was in a coma for more than four months. Since I came home, at the end of October 2003, I've been working on my rehabilitation process. I go to St. Vincent's Rehabilitation twice a week.

One of my greatest challenges has been with my memory. I have discovered that everyone has different memories of what happened in my past and sometimes their recollections do not match the ones that I have.

Now I'm finishing high school at Southport High School. I'm in an electric wheel chair. This restricts what I can and cannot do. Over the past two years, I have once again learned to breathe on my own, talk, type, write, feed myself, take care of some of my personal needs and now I am learning to walk once again. I do my best to try to stay healthy.

Before my accident I wrote poetry. It is 'my art'. It is what I did well. I always wanted to put my poetry into a book and now I have been given the chance.

About the Editor/Co Author

Hello, I am Mary. I am Michael's home tutor. I've been a teacher for a very long time.

I love to read. I've always wanted to write a book.

I've been very blessed to be able to work with Michael these past few years. I've been fortunate to be part of his growth and recovery. It's been very exciting. I've watched him progress from sitting and laughing at movies, to pointing to pictures, to typing his words, to talking with his trache, to breathing on his own, to seeing him independent in his electric chair and to see him walk with his walker.

Imagine my joy the day I walked into his house and his dad said, "Michael has a surprise for you." I turned to Michael and he spoke: "Hi Mary!" That was the first time he spoke to me!

We work very hard as he finishes his high school classes. I was impressed with his original poetry and saw how important it was to him to write as he progresses through recovery. We've used his writing to help him improve his language, his grammar and to explore his feelings as he recovers.

It is my great pleasure to help him publish his work.

It is my great pleasure to call Michael my friend.

www.ingramcontent.com/pod-product-compliance
Lightning Source LLC
Chambersburg PA
CBHW031230280526
45784CB00004B/1514

* 9 7 8 1 4 3 4 3 0 6 6 3 0 *